# THE STORY OF Ruth

Retold by **MAXINE ROSE SCHUR**

Illustrations by **GWEN CONNELLY**

KAR-BEN PUBLISHING

For my favorite Ruth, my mother Ruth Wolff—M.R.S.

Claudia and Evan Kamikow, may you never walk alone.—G.C.

Text copyright © 2005 by Maxine Rose Schur
Illustrations copyright © 2005 by Gwen Connelly

KAR-BEN PUBLISHING, INC.
A division of Lerner Publishing Group
241 First Avenue North
Minneapolis, MN 55401 U.S.A.
1-800-4KARBEN

Website address: www.karben.com

Library of Congress Cataloging-in-Publication Data

Schur, Maxine Rose.
    The story of Ruth / by Maxine Rose Schur ; illustrated by Gwen Connelly.
      p.  cm.
    ISBN–13: 978–1–58013–114–8 (lib. bdg. : alk. paper)
    ISBN–10: 1–58013–114–X (lib. bdg. : alk. paper)
    1. Ruth (Biblical figure)—Juvenile literature. 2. Bible stories, English—O.T. Ruth. I. Connelly, Gwen. II. Title.
    BS580.R8S38 2005
    222'.3509505—dc22                                  2004014265

Manufactured in the United States of America
1 2 3 4 5 6 – DP – 10 09 08 07 06 05

**L**ONG AGO IN THE LAND OF JUDAH A FAMINE CAME
upon the earth.  Wheat withered on the stalk.  Grapes shriveled
on the vine.  And fields once green as the sea now stretched dry
as dust all the way to Galilee.

In Bet Lehem, the town whose name means "House of Bread,"
there was no bread.  Nor meat, nor milk, nor wine, nor fruit.
Death, an unwelcome visitor, moved in and stayed.

Elimelech, a man of Bet Lehem, both noble and rich, said to his wife Naomi, "The rivers here run dry and no rain falls, but I hear that in Moab there is water and food for all who want it. Pack up everything; we will leave for Moab at sunrising."

Naomi's heart grew fearful. She did not want to leave everything she knew for a strange, faraway land. But she said nothing. She called her servants and her two sons, Mahlon and Kilion, to help her pack. They loaded the camels with wool blankets. They packed one large sack of raisins, one of dried fish, and their last urn of water.

When day broke, the little family set off on their
long journey. The way east wound around the
Dead Sea and through a desert the color of bone.
But they had food and water and each other.
By the new turning of the moon, they reached
Moab, a nation high on a plateau with fortresses
reaching toward Heaven.

Because the people of Moab were kind to her
family, Naomi's fear vanished and her heart was
like a freed bird.  Elimelech built a small house
at the edge of the plateau and there the family
began a new life.

But before the next harvest, Elimelech grew sick and died.  Soon after, Kilion married a Moabite woman with green eyes named Orpah, and Mahlon married a Moabite woman with black eyes named Ruth.  For ten years they all lived well. Then Naomi's sons, Kilion and Mahlon, took sick and died.

Hearing that in Judea the earth was again plentiful with food, Naomi decided to return to her own land. Naomi's daughters-in-law followed her for they loved her and were dutiful.

When they came to the desert, Naomi turned to them and said, "Go back, you cannot come with me. You are women of Moab and in Bet Lehem you will be strangers in a strange land. Go each of you to your mother's house! May God be kind to you as you were to the departed and to me. May God grant each of you a husband and a home in which you will find peace."

Naomi kissed each girl good-bye, but Orpah and Ruth wept, and their cries sailed into the hot silence. "Go back!" Naomi pleaded. "Go! My lot is too bitter for you! I am an old, poor woman now and must return to my people."

The daughters-in-law wept even louder, and this time their wails echoed off the barren rocks. Then, at last, Orpah kissed her mother-in-law and turned back toward Moab. Ruth did not move.

"Go back," Naomi said quietly to Ruth. "Follow after your sister-in-law."

Ruth stood still but her strong words flew fast. "Do not ask me to abandon you," she said. "For wherever you go, I will go. Wherever you stay, I will stay. Your people shall be my people, and your god, my God."

Naomi tried to speak, but Ruth would not let her. "Where you die, I will die, and where you will be buried, I will be buried." Then she added softly, "Nothing but death will separate us."

Ruth piled her blanket on the little donkey. Together, the two women slowly traveled on foot north through the barren wilderness.

One young. One old. Both strong.

**D**AY AFTER DAY THE MOUNTAINS OF MOAB
grew more distant as Ruth and Naomi turned slowly west.
At last they came to the Salt Sea, a huge lake so salty that
nothing in it could live.  It lay over the land as blue and still
as a second sky.

On their journey beside the lake, the sun burned the women so
that their skin became dry and red like the surrounding desert.
But at night when they stopped to eat, a cold wind blew up.
Then they would build a fire from acacia twigs, huddle together
for warmth, and fall asleep to the woeful howling of wolves.

When at last they reached Bet Lehem, Naomi and Ruth were
tired and hungry and dirty.  The townspeople came out to stare
at the two ragged women.

"That is Naomi," they said.  "Once she had a husband and
sons, a grand house with servants.  Once she had camels
and silks and gold and rubies.  Now she has nothing."

Ruth and Naomi pitched a tent at the edge of town and that evening Ruth said to her mother-in-law, "We will not beg for food. Now is the time of the barley harvest. I will go into the fields and glean. I will pick the shafts of barley that are leftover after the reapers, and from this we will have bread enough."

Naomi took Ruth's face gently in her hands and kissed her forehead. "Go, my daughter."

And so, at sunrising, Ruth set out.  When she came to a field that was larger than all the others, she asked the reapers if she could glean there and they agreed.  Quickly, she began to pick up the leftover barley stalks and tie them into bundles.  She did not rest and said little, for when she spoke, her words sounded strange in this new land.

All day, the sun burned down on the yellow fields but Ruth stopped only to wipe sweat from her face.

Before dusk, just at the moment when the hills look as if on fire,
Ruth noticed an older man dressed in fine blue wool watching
her.  She knew at once that the man was Boaz, the owner of the
fields and one of the great judges who ruled Judah.

"Listen my daughter," Boaz said to Ruth, "do not go to glean in
anyone else's fields.  I have told my men to do you no harm and
to fill vessels of water for you."

Surprised, Ruth asked, "Why should you care about me? I am only a poor foreigner."

"My men have told me how you have cared for your mother-in-law after your husband's death. You have left the land of your birth and come to us for refuge."

Then Boaz invited her to take dinner with him. In the shade of the cypress trees, they dined on tender lamb, juicy apricots, and cold, sweet cucumbers. Well after the ram's horn had signaled coming of night, Ruth returned to Naomi with the barley she had gleaned and some food she had saved from her dinner.

Ruth told her mother-in-law about Boaz. "I heard kindness in his words," she said, "and I saw kindness in his eyes."

"May he be blessed by God, who is ever merciful." Naomi cried, "Boaz is a relative of ours! Glean only in his field my daughter, for he is a great man and will protect you."

Ruth gleaned with the servants of Boaz for the rest of the harvest. From the barley, Naomi baked bread which she sold in the town. Naomi and Ruth now lacked neither food nor drink.

One evening, when the harvest was over, Naomi told Ruth to dress in her best clothes and to go to Boaz. "He will know what to do," Naomi said. "It is his duty as kin to marry you and give you children, so that our family name lives on."

Ruth was frightened but she did as her mother-in-law told her. That evening she smoothed olive oil on her slim, tanned body. She dressed herself in a gown of white linen, and about her head she wound soft scarves dyed with pomegranate and saffron.

She walked beside the great field of Boaz until she came to the threshing floor. Hidden in the shadows, Ruth saw Boaz and his servants winnowing grain.

When they finished, she watched Boaz eat and drink. Ruth waited a
long time, her heart pounding in terror that she might be discovered.
At last, the servants left, and Boaz lay down at the edge of the sheaves
to sleep. Silent as a gazelle, Ruth entered the threshing room and lay
at his feet.

In the middle of the night Boaz awoke and saw a
shadowy figure.  He jumped up.

"Who are you?" he demanded.
"I am your servant Ruth.  Spread the corner of your cloak
over me, for you are my next of kin."

"Bless you my daughter," Boaz said, "you have remained
loyal to me.  You have not sought a young man your own
age whether rich or poor.  All the people of Bet Lehem know
you are a worthy woman.  If you will have me, I will cherish
you forever...on the soil of Earth and in the sky of Heaven."

Ruth had never felt happier, yet in the next moment her
happiness dimmed for Boaz warned, "There is a kinsman
closer to you than I, but I will ask him to give up his right
to marry you."

The next morning Boaz went to the gates of the city and met the kinsman.  The man agreed to give up his right to Ruth. Boaz told the elders of the city of his plans to marry her. "May God make your new wife like Rachel and like Leah who built the House of Israel," they said.

Boaz and Ruth married and their love grew like fire.
Within a year, Ruth gave birth to a boy they named Obed.

Naomi loved Obed as if he were her own son. She cradled him in her lap and told him tales. He grew up strong and smart.

Obed's son was Jesse and Jesse's son was David, the first king of Israel.

THOUSANDS OF YEARS HAVE PASSED on this earth since David was king, and the Story of Ruth is still told. But it is not just the story of the great-grandmother of King David. It is more.

It is the story of Ruth and of Naomi who were blessed with the courage, the wisdom, and the might of women.

**Why do we read the Biblical book of Ruth on the holiday of Shavuot!**

Shavuot is an agricultural festival that celebrates the end of the barley harvest. The story of Ruth takes place during that season, and dramatizes the Biblical commandment of *leket* (gleaning)—leaving behind a portion of the harvest for the poor. At his invitation, Ruth gleans in the fields of Boaz, a wealthy landowner, who later becomes her husband.

Shavuot also commemorates the giving of the Torah. Moses brought the Jewish people to the foot of Mt. Sinai where they were given the Ten Commandments. The people responded, saying, "All that God has spoken, we will do and we will obey." In the same way, Ruth, a non-Jewish woman, made the commitment to become Jewish like her mother-in-law, and to accept the commandments of the Jewish religion.

Finally, Ruth is the great-grandmother of King David who, according to tradition, was born and died on Shavuot.